Pillow of Dreams

Dear Mom,

much love,

Pillow of Dreams

nivedita lakhera

*One hundred percent of this book's profits
will be used to develop telemedicine software
for people in need — in refugee camps, developing
countries, remote tribal areas, and acute disaster
situations.*

you cannot be
half a butterfly
and
half a caterpillar
for long

don't let
light scare you
just because
you are
used to darkness

trust the journey
and keep growing

the destiny
unfolds
but
takes its time

Published in United States of America
First printing, 2017

www.pillowofdreams.org
www.artwithacause.net

ISBN: 978-0-9984349-1-9
Library of Congress Control Number: 2017900149

Attention: Schools, Universities, Libraries and Businesses
The book is available at quantity discounts with bulk purchase for education, business or sales promotional use.
For information, please e-mail pillowofdreamsbook@gmail.com

give me
goosebumps
dear life
I don't want
to leave
untouched by you

When death made sense of life

Last year, my 38 year old patient died of metastatic cancer.

Yes, she was just 38.

How her life changed, for no fault of her own.

Incomprehensible,
I can't make sense of how perishable we are.

She admitted to having been postponing her life for a long time, just like most of us.

Despite severe pain gripping her every hour of every day, she wanted to live. Even with her swollen legs, patchy hair, severe back pain and near blindness, she wanted to hold on to life.

Her last wish was to go outside. For the longest time, she had been imprisoned in her hospital bed because of her pain and disease.

My compassionate intern and I wheeled her out to the first floor patio of our hospital. She died the next day... leaving a stubborn reminder of how we take life and people for granted.

I hope we live the life we truly want, say what we truly mean, be with those who we truly want to be with, and manifest the truth that we were born to manifest.

In truth, we find life, no matter how long or short.

Else, it's all just a sad lie.

Here is to never postponing living, and to never postponing our dreams.

Here is to acknowledging mortality with a vivacious spirit, living a life full of compassion for the self as well as others.

May your beautiful soul rest in peace.

This next poem is dedicated to you.

requiem

oh dear moment
slide slowly your fingers through her tresses
rest a bit on her eyes
before you dissolve in her mouth
as she tastes you complete
and you soak her words
like rain soaks the sea

oh dear moment
pause on her lips
for that eternal kiss
that lasts longer than a lifetime

be gentle and softly settle on her skin
before life exhales you out
as the very last one

let her capture you, in her lungs
on her canvas, in her song

she wants to feast on you
as a measure of forever
as the taste of sandalwood aroma
and the colors of fall
and the music of christmas lights
and the innocence of laughters
and the glow of bruised sunsets

let her travel through
the lil' garden of memories

oh dear moment part slowly
oh dear moment part slowly
oh dear moment part slowly

Dedicated to you, dear one.

This book is carved out of my soul.

Right here, right now, I feel close to you, so close that I can hear the crashing waves of your heart beating against my chest.

You are the one witnessing the unravelling of my soul and the disrobing of my mind within these restless pages.

Thank you for your sacred eyes and forgiving heart as you see all parts of me- truthful, naked, flawed, and real. I am giving you all of me here. I am kissing you with my shy words, caressing you with bold art, soaking you into my skin, exhaling away hurt in goosebumps, and finally dusting off your pain delicately, so you can witness all the glory of you.

Hold my hands, you are safe here. You very much belong here.

Here we celebrate your beautiful soul together, while putting wings on pain and embracing life.

As you start this journey you will find a lot of phrases surrounding you, touching your mind... playing with your hair... unraveling across your eyes as bits and pieces of laughter, a wave of goodbye, a forced smile, an honest tear, a face with a few words... a few faces with fewer words... curled between your toes as the sand of thoughts.

But then one of them will just jolt your soul, shiver your spine, and rearrange your view of the world, while stretching your vision beyond what you can see, making your sky more limitless than before. That poem is something that your heart would hug forever, that poem is a celestial word constellation that was created entirely for you in mind as the audience.

Keep on reading till that poem finds you!!

Thanks again for joining me here. I appreciate your softness.

Please send whatever extra love and forgiveness you have in your heart towards this imperfect but sincere attempt to reach out to you.

I love you so much. Welcome to this world of words. It's all for you and it's all yours.

namaste

nivedita lakhera

to be understood
is intimacy
of the highest level

contents

saibo

why love

because
that's all
I know

saibo

I love you
I don't know why
this life is not long enough
for that question

I'd rather collect your face
in my palm
and sleep in your dreams
and talk to stars
about how much
I am closer to you
than them

I'd rather chase the morning away
by pausing the indigo velvet sky
curled between my toes

as gods slow the clock
to witness beauty
of the hearts
when our eyes kiss

so I love you
and I will only
want to love you
in this
small forever moment
and the next moment
till time stops to count itself

ink me
said words
to feelings
I want to kiss
that lonely page
as poem

he knew
my words

I knew
his music

we were
the song
that love
danced to

it was
a scarf
you made
from very
fine moon-rays
I did the hem
with stardust
so we can wear
that night
when the heart feels
too much sun

in my jar of life
I have
a lot of fireflies
and
a smitten heart
full of you

love
a beautiful
reason
for the heart
to beat

she was not pretty
she was riveting
she was not a princess
she was a sphinx
she churned oceans
for her pearls
and she smeared rainbows
on her lips
but for him
she was just a girl in love

sona

like a still shore, l will await you
I will welcome both the pearls
and crashing waves of your heart

I will kiss your ascent towards the soft sky
and witness your rest
at the majestic horizons
I will celebrate
your seasons with the sun
and play with moon dust
and your liquid stars at night
I will welcome
your wrecks and dreams inside

I will be right there
as your stillness of everything
you can come and rock my sand
leave your treasure, wounds,
foams of anguish and dance of joy
in low tide, in high tide
and like a true lover

I will always welcome you
because your leaving has not left me
and your arrival has always arrived

you have crystallized in my soul
so I just send inch by inch of me
towards the sky to heave clouds
to pour me as restless rain
drenching your ocean waves

and exactly that's when
and exactly that's where
we are one
and I get to see
all of your depth

till then my love
like a still shore
I will await you

kiss me
one last time
I want
to remember
how to
breathe in
life again

that night
we made
an even swap
you gave me
a firefly
I gave you
my heart
now
you live in
all that is music
and I paint
the sky with
shimmering
stardust

the sliver of moon

you know my love
the sliver of moon
that gives just enough glow
to an indigo sky
wears the night
with so much pride
because it messages
lovers across
the petty distances
while trimming
the hems of clouds
with moonshine

I sent that to your window
to sing the romance
of all the hearts it carries
the yearnings of love
and the scourge of distance
all woven in the blanket of night
to keep your soul warm
and hopes alive

so let the dancing stars
glitter our songs forever
because the night is where
the world sleeps
and dreams awake and play
so my love
let us meet up soon
in the best of fairy tales

a single
ray
on you
and
I start
burning
like
a thousand
unsettled
stars
bursting
to touch
your lips

love stripped
her of her armor
then planted
more colorful seasons
than spring
then took her mind
to the rainbow slide
and seasoned her
with new words
she dived into new pages
which were
awaiting her ink
and then you ask
how she turned
into a song

that
semi- folded
moon
that shines
through
your dimples
my sky
wants to
claim him
for
all of my nights

I dived

into those

shallow

eyes

only

to get

drowned

in the

infinite depth

they

hide

so well

in
his
book
of
alphabets
she
was
the
only
song

violet

to greet your tender lips
I flew in with the restless breeze
and waited for eternities
in the soil as a dormant seed

with the rain of spring years
the branch turned all supreme
and caressed our pining sun
so bloom can come to me

flaunting all coyish petals
I hide my soft liquor
so your eyes can pluck me sweet
and celebrate my soft nectar

as I finally swell with the kiss
settling in warmer breath
that moment is eternity
in the life of a wild flower

one warm
touch of love
and her scar
became
a heart again

you
are
the promise
that
light made
when
I was
fumbling
through the dark

one more night

I spilled myself in your arms
and your eyes collected me delicately
first my heart and then my soul
wrapping the rest of me tenderly
your touch waltzed up
my heart then longed
in a song of love with no ending
and you tripped on eyes
flooded with want
all vision thus rested
till morning

for a velvet kiss
of one more night
I live my life in eternity
sharing a sunrise
just one more time
in the lap of lovely serendipity

the space
between
love and life
is the journey
of a most
restless story

our kiss

first you shred
what pain had weaved
and then you washed
all the rusty stains

then with magic
and silky threads
you made me a quilt
more like band-aid

and then you tore
all iron walls
and made a home
with soft petals

and broken glasses
don't hurt no more
they shine instead
like a chandelier

and all bruises old
feel like sunsets
they color my sky
with ombré shades

and I look behind
as we sail in the kiss
bidding goodbye
to all what- ifs

sinking in the clouds
of my lovely dream
we rain in the light
of a rainbow theme

I serve you tonight

a sacred moon
with several gems
an ounce of music
with rain that fell

a soft shoulder
with a stronger heart
a sachet of joy
radiant as pearls

the last ray
the first ray
and all in between

the grey the red
and the blue supreme
I serve you tonight
with a hope of dawn

a forgiving gaze
a healing song
come lie in petals
until the morn
when candles warm us
and love shines all

I serve you tonight
what all is divine
few dreams onto
chiseling of home
when candles warm us
and love shines all

free fall

I could not stop
as you fumbled in my eyes
and fell to my heart

what spark you set
causing lightning
in the clouds
of my dreams
lacerating across
the edge of my breath
setting fire in my veins
occasionally emerging
in me as goosebumps
till my delicate lips breathe you out

but some part of you stayed
as mist in my eyes
and a thousand kisses of rain on skin
and as a mural on my heart
and in the smile of lilies
and the touch of raindrop prelude

some of you stayed
as dance in my feet
and as the caress of moonlight
and the hope of dawn

most of you stayed
as music in my words
and stories on my canvas

and then I see you again
at the doorstep of my eyes

and then
there was
love
which made
sense of life
in the most
dizzy way

Dear one in love,

I am so very happy for you.

Your blessing is of unmeasured value. Love is heavenly because it frees the limits our known existence imposes. You are where life can transcend through physical flesh and greet the soul directly, an experience like living in a temple of innocence, where your faith in the beauty of life is restored.

Where, even though all the doors of all your senses are open, for some reason only magic enters to worship the heart.

While all of us are born with the power to love, a few lose our courage to do so till we are rescued by the playfulness of transient time and another glorious soul.

May a thousand words shine on your heart so each heartbeat becomes a song, and may it be so sacred that it becomes a prayer of love, for all the gods.

So hold on to the one you love.

The one who makes your mornings more peaceful, the one who stays with you like a dance of life, the one that is your rock, the one who both challenges you and comforts you. The one who helps you grow, but also rejoices in who you are.

There can be many destinations, many roads, many travels, but you will only need one home.

Enjoy this experience of the highest level. I hope it lasts a lifetime.

Remember, you see as much beauty as there is love in your heart.

So be in love and stay there.

namaste

nivedita lakhera

meera

his
name
was
her
favorite
song

crimson autumn

I sat in a little boat
of our thoughts
and sailed through
a very slow season
of cinnamon breeze
and red leaves

I revisited the island
where the crisp sun
held our hands
and we sipped
the music of chopin

and then I laughed
and your eyes smiled
as we plucked joy
from nowhere
and everywhere

we feasted
on the smell of sweaters
and the aromas of pumpkin
and devoured
the sultry world of words

and then we stood still
ignoring willfully
that life was longer
than that moment
it ran faster than
our tiny heartbeats

so we just planted
an autumn tree
and put a swing
on the most colorful branch
so we can see
our lovely
crimson leaves
lasting
through eternity

pain

surrendered

to

the army

of her music

she

set

it free

in her songs

you
were
my gravity
now
I just
float
through
life
holding on
to
our last dance

the only
moon I had
you
took that
away
now
all my nights
are at the mercy
of your stars

I refuse
to breathe out
all your
syllables
they are the ones
holding
my bleeding
flailing
rib cage
together

nothing consumed her
like the thought of him
but nothing really
brought her to life either
she loved
every inch of him
specially the parts
enameled with fears
she softened them
with her lips
and made her
shrine of love there

I set us
free
like
prayers
from lips
pious
desired
and
heartfelt

I am
exhausted
and
I have run
out of breath
and I still
cannot find
a single space
empty of you

her heart clued out
her missing piece
every time
she saw him
only with him
she felt
like a solved puzzle

entwined hearts

every inch of my skin
only sings to your touch
and the nape of my neck
is mapped with your lips
and I no longer remember
my very own breath
as it is entwined in yours

and my skin still carries
the fragrance of your embrace
and the color of my eyes is
still the glitter
your gaze left
when our souls collided

and my tresses
still bounce
and dance in the breeze
that may have
caressed your skin

and my flesh
warms up
in the cold shower
of rain
for somehow it may
have traversed
your heart first

and my face
tries to kiss the sun
that must be running
across your palm

and each night
still has silver stars
that borrowed twinkle
from the fireflies
that sparkled
when I soaked in your passion

so my love
yes my heart
still carries
the shrine of our love

serene seraph

crimson water
here you come
and kiss my fear away
where did that wave vanish
that promised to stay
frugal shells
left some dent
instead of
pearls in sand
tiptoeing
in the beach
of my heart
your footprints
met an end

and
once
again
he
flooded
her
heart
and
eyes
with
salty
water

your lips
were
my home
and now
I am
a gypsy
carrying
your
music
and
wearing
your
kiss

I bled
with storms
to tour
your heart
I fought
with the dragons
of your pain
to claim
its warmth
and now
I can't even find
my footprints
there

was
too much
and
then some more
a lot, lot more
he still
managed
to occupy
all of her

to kiss
your thoughts
my words
leap out
of my eyes
and then there is
always a
mortal touch
which leaves
much unsaid
so let me stay
in your mind
you post me
love letters there

I kissed you

my love

like the rain

kisses the sea

restless

chaotic

and completely

that's how

I lost myself

in you

I can't seem

to collect

my sober drops

amidst your massive waves

I just can't find me

I just can't find me

since I kissed you

my love

like the rain

kisses the sea

restless

chaotic

and completely

I hung
our moon
amidst the stars
of memories
to reach out
to you
each night
just so
you remember
our last kiss

when
the words
leave
meaning
promises
turn deaf

half a love
is a boat
towards
an island
of complete pain

love came in
like a tsunami
I wish
I knew
how to swim

I wanted to be
a flower
for a few days
do my dance
with the breeze
and finally
kiss the land
basking under
a lot of sun
I was that leaf
and
you were
my autumn

burgundy blues

in all colors of fall
I see nothing but us
we stole years from days
as we made defiant love

as our breaths rocked our pulse
and the fluttering light stayed young
and time paused and the rain cried
on our exquisite flesh with sweat

a thousand boats of memories
floated in the parting tears
a thousand promises were broken
as music in words was shred

in snowfall and in spring
our touch was a lovely song
it was a merry way
as romance waltzed with the heart

in all colors of fall
I see nothing but us
we stole years from days
as we made defiant love

purple song

a thousand stories
my eyes have said
and they sang
some lovely songs

but one is
where they made
a home
and refused to move along

the one
that had
the freshness of pine
and the fragrance
of the sandalwood
and the silky touch
of naive love
and the friendship
that was true

a thousand steps
my heart will take
on clouds of vast azure
and still dances
on music that glows
nostalgic undertones

strokes of separation

now what do I do with my aching heart
and pain so new with a wrath so raw
what do I do with my remaining love
as moments of us are memory now

how not to welcome spring with fair
and see you in music everywhere
to treat my red dress just the same
and still wear life with all its flair

each day learning to walk alone
and night, you need to just calm down
how do I let go of all my fears
and rescue strength from a pool of tears

I wake my dreams for an unknown dawn
as I tap my courage with a mighty straw
now what do I do with my aching heart
and pain so new with a wrath so raw

I don't miss you
but my tresses are rebelling for your arms
and my skin is thirsty for your mouth
I don't miss you
but my famished life and flesh
are living off the syllables of your name
absence of your touch is poverty to my soul

you

forgot

to

give

me

your

heart

with

your

words

Dear Broken One,

Here is the truth.

You are not breaking, you are getting refined.

It's very hard to see this truth when your eyes are drowning in salty water.

Pain is like love, it's powerful enough to make you shun every other sense with the capacity to take over and make you a hostage.

And so even if there is a massive crowd offering you love and life, you feel lonely. Because you are only lonely for that person who left a mountain of pain on your chest, where your heart used to beat with life, hope, and beauty.

That person filled your soul with a garden which left with him and now you are lying thirsty on a baking desert.

Your flesh is lifeless. Your heart has painfully cut your ribcage for a wild chase in a jungle of thoughts, running after the ghost of a gazillion questions.

And that chase will exhaust you even more. There is no cure, there is no shortcut. You will have to walk through that scary jungle filled with unkind thorns.

Breathing is going to feel like work to you. You would pray to sleep through the pain but that prayer will not be answered overnight, or even over several nights.

I cannot take that pain away, no one can.

But I am here to tell you that it's going to hurt a lot more for days, weeks, or months to come. Gradually, it's going to hurt a little less, and then much less, and then you would be plucking joy from nowhere and everywhere.

This longest night always happens before the most beautiful day. So hang in there in the hope of that day.

I am here to tell you that pain is a time travel towards unknown strengths you will not discover till you go through this dark time.

The most important thing that pain will do is give you the language of compassion. You will know next time when someone is hurting. You will understand each other like no one else. And this will become the source of strength for someone else when they need it the most. Trust me, your pain will save someone else's life someday. Your shattered heart will become the sponge for someone else's tears. And you will realize that you are that strongest warrior that you were looking for to rescue you. Hang in there. Please hang in there. It is really, really worth it.

Much love, from someone who is also broken, but a little less than the day before,
and much less than years before

namaste

nivedita lakhera

anahita

the softest words
filled up
the cracks in her soul
and that is where
poetry bloomed
to replenish
her stolen fragrance

right
in there
in the empty
bruised
closet
of
your soul
I am
gonna stack
my love
there

you are used to heart-crumbs
and half a love
you are used to dimming your sun
to match their moon
you are used to trimming your soul
to match the dimensions of their agreeable nods
you are used to borrowing their currency
to measure your own worth
except today
today my love you rise
and conquer the self

you are colors
beyond crayons
you are music
that has not existed yet
your vision
and your dimensions
are several light years ahead
you carry
a big bang in your heart
bursting celestial constellations
but the world next door
has area codes
you are a scripture
amidst people discovering alphabets
and then you wonder
why you can't be read
oh my darling you are special

a little of love
can save
a lot of you
and
a lot of them

let there be
no unwritten
love letters
let there be
nothing left
for tomorrow
let life
celebrate
in its entirety
and with completeness
a very sacred 'now'

don't you worry

oh my love
don't you worry
I picked up an extra smile for you
I also brought wings for pain
and a sponge for tears and disdain

I shopped some silky moments too
on my way
through life to you
and some silly reasons
for love as muse
and laughters from swings
without excuse
to stitch some warmth
for a time so chilly

oh my love
don't you worry

there is a lot of

hurt

I see

dripping down your smile

I am going to collect

all of it

to make

a most glorious collage

of your bravery

oh my love

your majestic warrior soul

deserves to see

the art it has created

over several years

sacred scars

I love your florid flaws
and delicate dark scars
and beauty oh so random
and refreshing like the dawn
you can weaken in my arms
with the rainfall of your heart
I see strength in all tears
and passion in your wants
you are power so unsaid
you will find you once again
It's better to be lost
than to stay in a lonely shell

you
are
forgiveness
and
that
is
the most
beautiful
you

a smooth journey
is rarely adventurous
you my love
with the heart of the lion
were not born
for sober quiet roads
but for the high of mountains
and the depth of oceans
so go ahead
and enjoy the hike

pain
will arrive
early
learning
will arrive
late
amidst
that space
is
the journey
you choose
and life
meets you
there

lullaby 1

you stride taller than any distance
with a vision defying all dark
your pain is a dot in the galaxy
of celestial compassion that you are
your stories are your lyrics
woven in the grandest music
you awake all dreams in life
unraveling your majesty

be
compassionate
towards
your
past
present
and
future

aakriti

one day you will find the words
words that a child recited
the child that you were once
invincible and never frightened

words that made all sense
not borrowed from the world
with vowels of your soul
truly and only yours

beneath the aging dust of 'ifs'
they still are shining brighter
they never left and sat beside
writing your valid address

one day you will find those words
words that a child recited
the child you were once
invincible and never frightened

they will give you
a measure
of pain and laughter
they will try hard
to trim your sunshine
they will call your heart
too much heart
and your love
too much love

no my darling
it's not you
you don't feel too much
but it's the world
that is numb with fears
you cannot crawl
when you are given
two majestic wings

so go ahead
and build a sky
for your generous flight

each
day
is
a
love letter
choose
beautiful
words

what
if
the
tiniest
of joys
are
celestial
then
we
have been
living
happily
ever after
all along

lullaby 2

trust me you are not
some sightless dreamless eyes
or flightless sorry bird
or fallen tempered skies

but yes my love you are
a light without a shadow
your power is unsaid
winning tides without a battle

mending lows with sultry highs
your warmth is a thousand suns
lending smiles for all the sighs
you share what all treasure

forget what they have told
stars kiss where you walk
and the sky becomes the floor
and songs become the talk

people
can't see
your pain
but they
will know
sooner
or later
what it
did to you
but more
importantly
what you
did with it
give your
heart
but keep
your courage

be
ample
be
enough
shine
on all
equally
like
a
florid
sun

once you

learn

to forgive

yourself

and others

an

undeniable

love story

between

everything

everyone

and you

will

commence

merchant of peace

oh merchant of peace you sell
you sell it hard enough
knock hard on hesitant doors
for coins of grudges so old
sell empathy to the soul
give love instead of charm
sell warmth for the lonely cold
addresses knowing just harm
new hope for those who fell
and a path to us all lost
sell no judgment with patience
and bandage for right and wrong
to the hesitant breeze of life
show it what is freedom
oh merchant of peace you sell
you sell a just kingdom

magic
lives
in the heart
dreams
just
whisper
about it

let me travel
through your dusty pages
that were never read

I will sing their glory
to you

we will
flaunt
them
together

so he broke your heart
so they broke your spirit
someone bled your back
someone betrayed your love
straighten your crown
and stride
like the lioness that you are
they are just noise
you oh my darling
you are one majestic song

make space
for
an
ounce of magic
in everything
you believe

no destiny is greater than thine
you dream of the sky and you must fly
your wings are vigorous bold and true
anoint new skies with your own blue
a warrior you are, don't you quit
you aren't just another slot to fit
make new colors and stroke ahead
rewrite the world with your paint
make your mark and don't be shy
no destiny is greater than thine

zenith

as her auburn hair waved
to the sky
jumping through hurdles
of this life
as her heart grew stronger
when it broke
imagination soared with
each tragic stroke
she fell and rose and she
breathed it all
she hiked the world
for the mountain top
she felt so light and
thanked her hope
she found it right and
worth the sweat
as she embraced the zenith
for the view was great
now she heal- fully cheers
for others in sight
as her auburn hair waved
in the sky

love thyself

for drinking voice from the bar of noise
and embracing the cashmere cloud of poise
for tasting dewy tears of 'let go'
and seeking finally 'what is you'
for sharing courage with any being
and shining grey winter with a colored spring
for loving all no matter who hurt you
and spreading your well earned divine hue
you deserve this glory not just today
but for beaming your hope everyday
for sailing bravely even in low tide
and for drinking voice from the bar of noise

create

conquer

celebrate

repeat

Dear one, the one gently healing,

As I smell sunshine in the young breeze of dawn, I feel the warmth of being alive.

That moment becomes one of the best moments of life, a simple uncomplicated pleasure.

All of us mortals feel pressures to achieve social milestones, so we can be recognized in the platforms where familiarity makes others feel safe to approach us, accept us, and make us a part of them.

But my love, it's so, so, so very vital to let your soul also manifest.

So I just want to give you a slice of your own life, to carve a little space in your life for only YOU. Where your soul shines through, to keep your light no longer hidden beneath others' expectations.

I ask you to take a mind vacation there, let your heart and soul wander in that beautiful place. **In that sacred space you will meet your passion.**

But when you find your purpose, please don't fall into the trap of worrying about whether or not you are recognized, accepted, or rewarded.

That is YOUR true address, where you are celestial. I want for you to take frequent trips to that place, till that becomes your home and the rest of the universe merely a neighbor.

Whether you win the entire world or some little hearts, to dust you shall return again.

So, my love, have fun with yourself, and your blessings. Go ahead and collect coins of happiness till you have so many that you can lend them selflessly to those around you.

Listen to your heart, trust your own mind, and kiss each moment which is as mortal as yourself.

And don't be scared once you start that journey.

Be fearless and indulge in every experience, every encounter; in everything that makes you feel something. Anything that you let pass through your soul is creating a gateway towards the light of the cosmos within.

Bathe in that light and it will soak away all the darkness that is the 'unreturned gifts' of the unwanted past.

You are doing great. Go ahead & live in the beauty of your heart.

And don't forget to be kind to yourself.

namaste

nivedita lakhera

mulan

dive

in your

own

wildfire

and

you will

never need

the sun

again

at times
life chooses for you
your path
and people

but you choose
how much
you celebrate
and forgive them

I say
celebrate them hard
and forgive them hard

life is too little
and too short
not to have
that intensity and zest

till
she
faced
her
heart
she
never
owned
her
eyes

you have
no control
over what they do to you
but I promise
you have full control
over what you do
to yourself

so my darling
tell me now
how are you
building up
your lovely self
today

lake of no sunsets

no rainbow will curve its smile
till the sun shines on the hesitant rain
all clouds will lose their shades
lest mist sip on warmer rays
for all your held up tears
my eyes are sultry lakes
I will keep your autumn fog
you keep my summery days

I hope you never see
your antique dreams
in the nostalgia shop
I want you wearing them
big bright and beautiful
breathing with you

lullaby 3

you are the fire
no one can burn you down
you are the river
no one can drink you down
you are the sun
no one can stare you down
you are celestial
no one can hold you down

your pretty
has a void
your scars
have depth
your pain
has compassion
and your zest
has the whole of my heart

I will bend time
to make
a massive swing
to grab
all of my
stardust
for your
lightless sky

let hope
tickle
your soul
and all
hesitant smiles
would be freed

it's ok

it's ok to be wounded
it's ok to be naive
it's ok to still be willing
and smile big and bright

it's ok to be hopeful
amidst all disapproval
it's ok to dream strong
when you are feeble

it's ok to be sad
tasting tears unknown
it's ok to be fearful
of what lies beyond

keep walking lovely heart
with mind soul and strength
how amazing the journey was
you shall find in the end

let
the fire
that
burns you
become
an eternal light
for all

and one day
you won't just
collect your pieces
but will make
a massive chandelier
out of them
to lay glitter
on the lightless skies
of others
and that's
what makes
that most
untold fairy tale
a most
beautiful one

oh my lovely
majestic
princess warrior
your pain
will sharpen
your compassion
and that is all
you will need
to win hearts

she tried to peel
fear off her skin
but it was drilled
deep into her bones

so she dipped herself
in a pool of passion
and fear melted away
like jazz in the air

she glowed that day
like
a thousand suns
and she
never never never
stopped since then

deal with it

how many books you wrote
just to mark territory on my body
how many versions of shame you stitched
to mask my voice
how long a list you crafted
for dos and don'ts for my walk
how many whispers you collected
to shun the length of my skirt
how many eyes you glued to my skin
to be a stop sign for my road
and set standards for my grace

and still today
I carry an ocean of passion
no your rules
will never contain my tsunami
or extinguish the sun of my eyes

your hungry throats
won't drink down
my river of sandalwood fragrance
you cannot tame
the bounce of my tresses
and the roaring of my soul

your blotchy judgement
has no place in my wisdom
your noise cannot cover
my hard earned victory song

I am a woman
I am a majestic warrior queen
I am a goddess of my land
courage is my scripture
even my silence
carries the drumroll of life

I have a mighty pen
with a lion's heart
to write my own story
and rule my own destiny
deal with it

I bust the windows

I made a collage
of our broken glass
to put on the wall
that drifted afar
it still cuts through
my tender heart
but I see where
I have come so far
I danced to all
the faintest tunes
I saw deserts
and I saw dunes
I handed my heart
to life so fine
rested in palm trees
and kites up high
you must have thought
I would stay curled in
in our room
furnished with lonely sighs
but I burst the wall
with a window strong

I stitched my wings
and then I fled
forgave the time
that had me lie
no more I walk
but free I prance
I am glad I gave
my life it's chance
on my way to love
I dropped all scars
and that's how my dear
I have come so far

new horizons are new homes

I caressed away my pain
and my light shined within
as breeze whisked all the clouds
and the curvy moon was seen

I awake to 'all that is'
and closed the dusty book at last
I sailed towards the sun
leaving the island of the past

and I drowned and drenched and danced
in the rocky waves of the sea
my hair glistened and eyes spoke
that's a fairytale to me

I did not look behind
past glaciers my boat just swooned
and time became my song
as new horizons formed new homes

healing pain

if I were a feeling
I would be compassion
for a destination
I would be redemption
for a florid revenge
I would be forgiveness
for a generous time
I would be in no haste
for an innocent smile
I would be a gentle pace
for being an army
I would be the desert rain
if I were a blessing
I would be healing pain

when you are a true lover
to all your darkness
in good marriage
with your bronze freckles
when you are loyal
to your own raw red core
mocking acceptance and rejection alike
hammering windows to uncertain recesses
to invite the bright golden sky
for a hot tea time with your soul
that's when you are truly home

soar

withheld before she jumped
in the air to do her dance
refrained before released
a bird flapping so hard
on the edge of life and dream
a bridge of action lies
it may be an ocean or a desert
she can't know staying inside
water will make her swim
and sand will teach her to build
in the air to do her dance
she refrained
and then released

refuse

I refuse to be an opinion
refuse to be mired mistakes
refuse to be a sum of past events
refuse to be just a name
for I am the wild of the wind
that flows where the sky is mine
where all the rainbows sing together
and more than one sun shines

I refuse to hold the dreary past too long
or tempering 'what will be'
I am a moment
I am my truth
and a song of several whims
a heart of music
and feet with wings
awake to see within
roar fly and run to seek
I am the calm of a silent beat
to dance sing and to taste it all
I don't need to just belong
refuse to be an opinion
or to live as a mortal want

boundless

I choose
my lightheartedness
over your measured
heavy frowns
I choose
the froth of art
between my toes
over your safe fountain
I choose
the taste of naive songs
in my mouth
over your verbal math
I choose my trying light
over a borrowed vision
I choose my getting lost
over your cautious maps
I choose me this time
and I am going to choose me
next time and next- to- next time again
over your preferred version of me

loneliness is a
failed introduction
to the cosmos within
solitude is
a mesmerizing
journey into that

imperfect light

I am neither all the answers
nor made up of 'rights'
I am the sum of many mistakes
and several more in sight

I'll keep burning till the end
as a candle which won't quit
and will defy the winter
however grey and grim
I know short is my life
and small may be my light
I'll keep calming what is dark
like the dewy moon at night

it was not

about

what

she dreamt

but what

she dared

and that

became her

a silent war

was

fought

between

the road and

the heart

new dreams

were

conquered

without

bloodshed

the last piece
of the lie
was
the heaviest
but
truth
gave her a hand
and
she
got rid of it

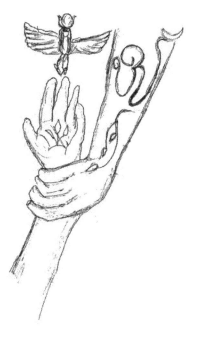

the tsunami
craved for her
she was
the adventure
that water
awaited

courage
the
only
way
to see
the
most
glorious
version
of yourself

there was no way
for her
to say it all
and to be with it all
so she grabbed her fire
and fled for the skies
and then she rained hard
with all her hearts
all her passions
words songs and colors
she rained
on all the lands

her scars
were
prettier
than her
dewy skin
they were
enameled
with gushing stories
full of
highs lows
and glitches
they were a book
that life
wrote on her

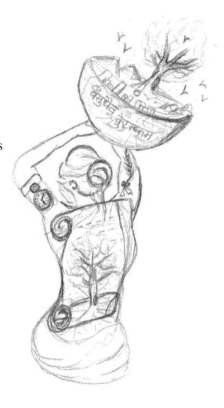

she flirted
with words
they fell in love
with her music
the cosmos was not ready
for such songs
but art was

free wings

honorable pearl you shine
I belong to fugitive wings
I see your elite shell
I belong to sultry dreams
a beautiful day is born
a new moment appears to kiss
not wondering as you said
but exploring is my bliss
so much to taste and devour
shells are just lovely locks
I am a coal of fiery passion
you collect symmetric rocks
I am the wildest of my wild
why seek order in my whims
honorable pearl you shine
I belong to fugitive wings

there was
no mortal comfort
in her wild fire
but the tiny sun
was not enough
to brighten
all of her
farthest horizons

she
unwrapped
her wings
from
the heavy cloak
of shame
to drink
her sky
and to dance
with fireflies
and to ride
the shooting stars

the seduction
of possibilities
with
each sunrise
is addictive

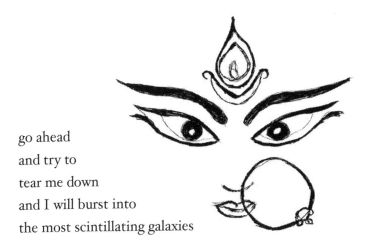

go ahead
and try to
tear me down
and I will burst into
the most scintillating galaxies

you want to set me
on fire
but darling
I am a fire eater

you want to bury
my flesh
under the massive earth
but I will come out as
the dense sandalwood forest
to home my own kingdom

oh my darling
I am energy
and only love can contain me

dance
to exhilarating conversations
between your heart mind soul
and their
romance with ideas

listen
to the passion of the universe
that whispers to you
in the form of your dreams
and travel to act on it

oh
will that bring suffering
yes it will
but it will be entirely yours
and if you keep a clean intent
it would be followed by joy
which would be innate

I promise
beyond the fire- wall of fear
there is a world which is all yours
and that my darling
is your one true address

the sparkle
in her eyes
was a gift from the moon-dust
and the glitter of her smile
was the destination of
the shooting stars
she kissed the dark with light
to seal the broken heart
and it worked like magic
every single time

she
shrunk
herself
to
fit
his
heart
but
her
dreams
kept
spilling

she refused to be
a serene picture

she was
a patchwork
and
a collage
of several stories
a book
not a snippet

but only a few knew
how to read that

there was
nothing
lukewarm
about
her fierce passion

it would simmer
an entire ocean
with a mere gaze

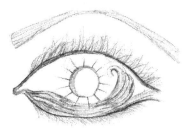

be a goddess
that you are
not a victim
no one can steal
light from sun
be boundless
you are limitless

because
I am
made of colors
and you ask
why
my canvas
is so bright

you
can't see
your rainbow world
without
having
both mist and light
in your lovely eyes

there will always be
something or someone
that will rotate your soul
crush your faith
parch your lips
off your dreams
simmer the skeleton
of your very existence

and exactly that's when
and exactly that's where
your destroyed land
will flourish with
the most beautiful garden
that your hope rescued

I will drive
the sky crazy
with my own blue
and the ocean
is yet to learn
my depth

emily

I dwell in possibilities
of heart mind and soul
in the restless untouched shore
at the naïve hope's abode
and the sky plumed with a sun
with a festive life's hum
of cashmere stir- less moon
in a vivacious dream's womb
I dwell in possibilities

I lost
my summer
to autumn
my leaves
were
ready
to kiss
the land

no one will hand over
your purpose to you

it's hidden behind all the walls
enameled as 'impossible'

over and over and over again
beneath all the falls
that your fear will scare you with

and it will reveal itself
only when you dive into your own wildfire
and want it more than life itself

give me your pain
and I will give you a poem
give me your sufferings
and I will tell you stories of
your bravery you did not know
give me your darkness and
I will show you the undying sun
that burns in your eyes
you are the universe
that you have not travelled yet
I am here to show
what massive constellations
you have created
just by being yourself

Dear Majestic Warrior,

The undying twinkle in your eyes will always shine your road ahead.

It's your little visions that will make a light to fight darkness in the most humble yet powerful ways.

For there will always be a path that your soul will carve through mountains of impossible, and that, my darling, will lead to the greatest adventure that your heart seeks and life celebrates.

Because the best part of getting lost is finding an unexpected journey and discovering an even more amazing version of yourself.

Like a shooting star, traverse your sky and unleash your glow. I promise, the glimpse of you will fight the darkness for at least one soul that needs it the most.

Keep burning, keep shining, let the light flow.

Remember, you will always be more than the noise around you, and taller than the ceilings of resistance. Remember to be you, and remember you are all those things and much, much more.

Along this journey a few wars will be given to you to conquer the self. Those are the battles worth fighting.

Let the fire that burns you become an eternal light for all.

I am so proud of you, remain glorious.

namaste

nivedita lakhera

my lil' love letter to you...

I am a stroke survivor, divorce survivor, and a heartbreak survivor.

This book is a much needed rendezvous, where we needed to meet each other to love together, to laugh together, to travel together, and to heal together.

These pages, at times tearfully crafted, at times joyfully crafted, but always hopefully crafted, are an attempt to sit next to your heart, and to have a conversation with your feelings; feelings that you have locked away in the cold recesses of your soul because of silly or sincere fears.

Let me open those bruised boxes—where your pain has been left unattended- with the sunshine of kindness, so that the fog of the past is replaced by the spring of the present.

I invite you to rest with me on the *Pillow of Dreams* for a few moments, amidst the massive race of life.

I truly hope, as every single poem in this book is woven, that it becomes a colorful, soft, and tender blanket for your soul.

Thank you for being with me all through this journey.

Don't forget to be kind to yourself & others.

namaste

nivedita lakhera

about the author

Born and raised in New Delhi, India, Nivedita Lakhera grew up in a very loving and supportive family.

At age 27, her life was jolted and derailed by a massive stroke, followed by a divorce, and then a heartbreak.

She turned to words and colors to rescue her soul. And, oh yes, they did rescue her. And now she wants to share them with everyone.

Pillow of Dreams is her first poetry book. She sincerely believes that, beyond the realms of time, class, opinion, birth, and religion, all of us are connected by the common threads of love, loss, joy, sorrow, betrayal, support, and friendship. And so a poem, a verse, a phrase, becomes a temple where anyone can visit and rest their souls before embarking on the next journey. A retreat and oasis of belonging and familiarity...that all hearts beat the same!

She is a medical doctor who is passionate about helping underserved people gain medical care via technology. Towards that goal, she is developing a telemedicine platform and a universal electronic medical records (EMR) which will be used to provide medical care in Syrian refugee camps, acute disaster situations, and remote areas in developing countries. She is using this book to raise awareness and funds for this effort.

She can be reached at pillowofdreamsbook@gmail.com for questions about her upcoming poetry book and mission.

about the art in this book

The painting on the **front cover** was the first mixed media artwork created as a part of a series called *Mulan* by Nivedita Lakhera. The *Mulan* series expresses feminine struggles, endurance, victories, chaos, failures, and calm via both colors & poetry.

Exhibited and sold at the Red Dot Art Fair during *Art Basel* in Miami, the painting got a lot of attention and was celebrated amongst viewers hailing from all walks of life.

Ms Lizzette Jacobson, a passionate art lover from Chicago, purchased the painting. Her description of the painting as having given her an instant spiritual experience echoes comments from other viewers.

The green strip near the margin on the **back cover** was created by a young boy living in a Syrian refugee camp in Greece. The author met him during a trip to the camps, assessing telemedicine implementation. While there, she also wanted to spread the warmth of color by bringing art supplies and painting with kids, in their cold, cold times of struggle.

All **interior sketches** were created to unfold a visual extension of the poetry, leading to a more textured, emotive, and multi- dimensional experience throughout the book.

The author created the original sketches with ball point pen on white office paper, in moments of reflection. The autographed original artwork and paintings are available for sale at www.pillowofdreams.org, and at Dr. Lakhera's online art gallery, www.artwithacause.net.

Made in the USA
Columbia, SC
21 June 2017